LIFE IS GOOD

WIT & WISDOM FROM A VERMONT HOMESTEADER

Nancy Carey Johnson

Honeyberry Books

POULTNEY, VERMONT

Nancy Carey Johnson/Honeyberry Books
www.nancycareyjohnson.com

Cover Design Gus Yoo
Copy editing and production Stephanie Gunning
Book Layout © BookDesignTemplates.com
Author photograph Matthew Pirrone

Life Is Good/ Nancy Carey Johnson. —1st ed.

ISBN 978-0-578-54866-1

Though richer
hardships — life truly
is Good!

To Forrest, Hunter, Wilder, North—and Jolly

Happy Reading

Nanny Carey Johnson

CONTENTS

Introduction

Funny how things go in life. I grew up in Brooklyn and spent summers in the country at my grandparents' house. And while there is much to recommend the city, I always knew that I didn't belong there and that I would be *much* happier living in the country.

After college, I worked in a green market by Union Square in Manhattan. Eventually, I met a man from Upstate New York, married him, and moved to a place on the map where the Hudson Valley and Berkshire Mountains meet and began country living in earnest. Along the way, we raised four sons and were adopted by our dog, Jolly.

Looking back at my life, I realized that the adage "Life is about the journey, not the destination" genuinely applies to me. I've worn many hats in my life: wife, mother, homesteader, chief cook and bottle washer, gardener, forager, singer/songwriter, friend, and volunteer, along with "holder of an eclectic array of jobs." Of late, I'm hemp farming.

I am also an accidental writer. Meaning, until recently I'd never in my whole life considered myself to be, or aspired to be, a writer. And it took a fourteen-year-old girl to point out that I was a storyteller, when she said, "Oh, another one of Mrs. Johnson's famous stories!"

I started writing my stories on Facebook when a friend complained about all the regurgitated memes and hateful political posts on social networks these days that were constantly appearing in her feed. She pleaded with her friends and acquaintances: "Tell me about your day. About the things you saw and did today. About your life." And so, I did.

Funny thing, after I started doing that, I gained "readers," people who for years, encouraged me to write a book. I put them off until finally, somebody said, "No, really. You should." That's when I rolled up my sleeves and went to work. It turns out that I now have enough material for several books.

Life Is Good is the first of several I have planned. I hope you enjoy it!

Nancy Carey Johnson
August 2019

Life Is Good

1. A Real Woman

I think I can finally call myself a "Real Woman." No doubt you are rolling your eyes as you read this but hear me out.

When I was a kid, I learned to kill cockroaches with my bare hands. THWACK, one hard, well-placed hit and *voila,* dead.

Then I overcame my fear of spiders. Don't ask me how. I don't know. Nor do I know why, only that I did.

But the realization hit me that I just might have earned the title of Real Woman when my slug traps didn't work (more on that another time) and I finally screwed up my courage. Now I kill *those* slimy things that are destroying my garden with my bare (SQUISH, POP, DONE) hands!

Think I might be ready to tackle my fear of worms.

2. Early Morning Diner

Got up and brewed my first cup of morning tea in a mug my favorite Aunty Luce gave me years ago. On either side of it on a bright orange background there is a gold half sun and underneath it emblazoned with large, bright yellow letters on a black background are the words, "Bright and Early Diner." Below all of that, in small black letters on the white background of the rest of the mug, it says, "We're Never Closed."

This mug resonates with me. I *love* to be up early mornings and watch the sunrise (yeah, I know, what kind of crazy musician am I anyway?) but it's true. My very favorite part of the day is early morning and more than that, I *love, love, love* to be on the road *early* before the sun's risen, watching as the world comes alive from the perspective of the road.

I'm not entirely sure *why* that is, only *that* it is, but if you add an early morning blow-in to a truck stop diner where you can grab a cup of coffee, a glass of juice or a quick breakfast, I am one happy camper!

3. Faith Rewarded

I've tried. In fact, I've tried for years to no avail. And then the other day I was in my garden doing something or other when the white caught my eye. I couldn't believe it and did a double take! Then I walked over and took a closer look, to be sure.

And there, right there, plain as the nose on my face was a head of cauliflower. Not a very big one mind you, but it was quite a bit bigger than a softball. I started looking around and realized that in fact, I had several heads of cauliflower, each of them considerably smaller than the first one that caught my attention, but all cauliflower none-the-less.

I'd been toying with the idea of pulling out their big stalks all summer because, for yet another season, they were sitting there taking up space doing nothing, but there is something in me that doesn't allow me to pull things that might, just *might*, grow into something.

I think that's called faith. And while my faith may not look like other people's, I am blessed with a ton of it.

4. And God Said, "Thwack"

Once when I was performing at a music festival, I invited a friend to join me on stage for a few songs. One of the songs we sang was the gorgeous old Scottish folk tune dating back to the 1600s "The Water Is Wide" (or "Waly Waly"), on which we sang a duet.

Afterward, a woman from the audience rushed up to us and said, "That was *the most beautiful thing* I've ever heard! It was so beautiful it made me cry!"

She paused for a moment in silent contemplation. Then, as we were basking delightedly in this amazing revelation, she continued, "Or I dunno ... maybe I cried because my grandfather just died."

Yeah, one of those moments when you got thwacked in the head just as you're feeling pretty good.

5. Shackles and Chains

I n my typical tomboy fashion, I don't collect things like Hummel figurines or dolls—not me! Nope, I like things made of iron. Specifically, heavy iron. Like old ice tongs, ancient honest-to-God clothes irons, old barn hinges, and the like. I even cook using old, heavy, cast-iron pots and pans. Well, you get the idea.

One day at a flea market, I came upon a table piled high with all sorts of cool and curious wrought-iron doodads! I was in my glory. I was like a baby seeing a Christmas tree full of lights for the first time and not knowing which light to look at first! I spent quite a bit of time at those tables, poking around and studying the gorgeous pieces of human invention and having a hard time deciding which piece I was going to gift myself

Finally, I chose a cool-looking piece. It is six inches long and on the bottom is a small (one-inch-diameter), solid, heavy ring attached to a three-inch split shank. As this goes up, it forms an oval circle (four-inches from side to side) that splits at the top. Two heavy iron balls are affixed where the ends of the circle meet. Also, on the shank between the small bottom ring and the top ring that opens, on either end, there is heavy-gauge wire attached to what looks like washers. You can open the top circle by squeezing the washers together and compressing the wire. For a tomboy like me, this tool was heaven! I gladly lugged my purchase around for another couple of hours and when I got home, displayed it proudly on my wall!

One day, as a friend who was visiting was examining it, she turned to me and said, "So tell me, why exactly is it you have a bull ring on your wall?"

Welcome to my world.

6. Pickled Leeks

Yesterday, as I helped myself to some pickled leeks that are stewing in one of the crocks that live on my counter, I found myself vaguely thinking about canning—putting things up for the winter—and all that goes with it.

I *love* having a crock full of pickled things on my counter. It takes me back to when I was young and the wonders of good, old-fashioned pickle barrels. You could get super sour pickles the kind that makes you pucker just thinking about them, or the really flavorful, but not so puckering half sours. And there's something about a crock full of pickles on a counter that's inviting; I get such pleasure when my family and friends dip into the crock with a slotted spoon or a pair of tongs and either pop a few pickles in their mouths or put them more daintily on a plate to devour.

Because you can pickle just about any vegetable, I keep sundry pickles on the counter depending on the season. Right now, it's the pickles made from leeks I foraged a few weeks ago. The batch before was pickled beets I'd purchased in bulk. Soon there will be pickles made of cucumbers from my garden.

It occurs to me that I've never pickled green tomatoes. I'll have to try that come harvest season.

7. Kitchen Dancing

Recently I've been playing Neil Young's "Harvest Moon," which has led me to think about one of my all-time favorite pastimes, kitchen dancing.

I think it was the beautiful corn broom in the music video of the song that is both sweeping and keeping time as people are dancing that reminded me of sweeping my kitchen, and of course, dancing.

When my boys were little, we would frequently and spontaneously start dancing in the kitchen. Sometimes there was music playing. Sometimes we'd make our own music and sing our own songs. When they were very little, they would hug my knees and start to dance, and then I would pick them up and twirl them around so their feet would be flying out and away from their bodies. Then I'd bring them in, and we'd dance.

As they got older, I showed them how to hold a lady properly when they danced, and also things like the in and out swing of '50's style dancing—and the next thing we knew, we were off! Usually, we'd make up steps as we'd go, and truth be told, I don't remember a whole lot of rhyme or reason to how we danced, but we sure had fun!

Kitchen dancing also was just about my favorite part of our Christmas Eve celebrations! I'd make some nice finger foods and a lovely, albeit simple dinner and we'd sing, talk, laugh, eat, and kitchen dance.

Sorry to say, my large, lunkheaded boys, now in their twenties, are no longer interested in kitchen dancing with their mother. But believe me, all those memories live *very* close to my heart.

8. Early Morning Riser

It was late last night—1:00 am—before I got to bed. Then I was awakened at 4:45 am by a bird singing right outside my window, no doubt saying, "Come on, lazy bones, time to get up!" And because I am a crazy woman, I obeyed the bird's demands.

I am an early riser by nature, and I *love* this time of year when daylight breaks by four and the sun has risen by five. I love how the world is starting to come alive, so very gently, at that time of day and how I don't have to wait hours for it to happen.

Soft early morning glow, birds singing, bugs chirping and humming, cool air gives way to warmer air with the scents of spring enveloping you. It's so peaceful, and a great way to "come to," as it were.

Forrest is still visiting and, as I sit here writing, sipping a hot cup of tea with milk and honey, and reveling in the cool morning air, I've got two dozen blueberry muffins baking in the oven as a Sunday morning surprise.

There are so many things that I can no longer do or take care of for my boys. They are all young men and must meet the demands of their lives and learn for themselves the lessons life has to offer. And while it is hard for me to sit by and watch, I know that is the role to which I'm now relegated.

Something I *can* offer, however, is the comfort of home and memories of youth. And one of the best ways I know how to do that is to have my house redolent from scents of delicious things, like blueberry muffins baking in the early morning, just as I did when they were little. So, I am.

Life is good.

Nancy's Blueberry Muffins

These never last long on the counter at my house.

Time: 35 minutes
Yield: 1 dozen muffins

Ingredients

2 T flour, for dredging berries
1 cup blueberries
1-1/2 cups flour
3/4 cup sugar
1 tsp baking powder
1 tsp baking soda
4 T salted butter, melted (if you use sweet butter, add
    a pinch of salt)
1/4 cup milk
2 eggs, scrambled
1 cup sour cream

juice and zest from a half lemon (or 1 tsp almond
    extract or vanilla extract)
butter for greasing the muffin tins (optional, if you're
    not using paperback muffin cup liners)

Instructions

1. Preheat the oven to 350 degrees.

2. In a small mixing bowl, dredge the blueberries in 2
    tablespoons flour and set aside.

3. In a large mixing bowl, whisk all the other dry
    ingredients together (flour, sugar, baking powder,
    baking soda).

4. In a saucepan, melt the butter over a low flame—do
    not burn. Add the milk and warm it—do not scald.
    Whisk to combine. Let cool for a few minutes.

5. Add butter/milk mixture, scrambled eggs, sour
    cream, juice of ½ lemon, and your flavoring of
    choice (either lemon and lemon zest, or almond or
    vanilla extract) to the large bowl. Using a wooden
    spoon, combine the batter thoroughly with as few
    strokes as possible.

6. Gently fold the dredged blueberries into the batter.

7. Fill *well-greased* muffin tins or paper-lined muffin
    cups to ¾ fullness. Bake for 25 minutes.

Enjoy muffins warm or cool, with or without butter or
jam.

9. It's Official

Ha! I guess I've officially joined the ranks of Old Ladydom. Because I've started carrying things around in my bra when I have no pockets— like the timer that my dear friends Randy and Sharmon gave me. This way, I can be outside in the garden and still know when the cookies are done!

My eldest son, Forrest, is coming up this weekend, so I'm making a *large* batch of coconut chocolate chip shortbread. I *know* the *first thing* he'll do when he walks in the door is make a beeline to the cookie jar.

With the way things change so quickly in this life, I am *so glad* that some things stay the same!

10. Noon Whistles

I was outside with Jolly, putzing around in my garden, when I heard what is music to my ears: the noon whistle. I *love* noon whistles. I grew up with them marking the time of day. Though I have no idea of their true origins, I've always assumed they were invented to let everybody know it was time for lunch—or at least that's what I thought when I was younger. And let me tell you, this little girl's day wasn't complete unless she heard the noon whistle!

I used to listen for it, though I wasn't always sure if it was the noon whistle sounding or a call to an emergency, and then I'd have to run and check the time. For a while, when my boys were little, we lived a quarter-mile from a firehouse, and so we were *very aware* of both noon whistles and emergency sirens. When my boys heard the noon whistle, they'd come running to me like Pavlov's dogs, telling me it was time for lunch!

18

For me, noon whistles have a similar essence to the old-time night watchmen who would walk through towns and villages preventing crime, noticing fires, helping drunks home, waking people who needed to rise early, and on the hour yelling out things like, "Ten o'clock and all is well!" Charming and reliable. Not a bad thing to be in this crazy world!

A reminder of the passing of time, both past and present, I hope noon whistles will continue to be part of our collective consciousness always.

11. Woodchuck

For the last year or so, I've taken to carrying around a half-gallon mason jar of water, because I don't want to drink out of plastic containers anymore if I can help it.

But I noticed I've been getting a lot of really funny looks from all sorts of people that I didn't understand until somebody said, "Holy crap, that's a *lot* of 'shine you're drinking!"

That hadn't even *occurred* to me.

I'm such a woodchuck.

12. Performance Art

I've never really understood performance art. I guess it's because I'm not cool enough, but even having said that, there was a time when my boys were young that I did have an idea for a performance art piece I could do. Though truth be told, I'm not sure if that term applies.

Day after day, I'd haul stuff out the pockets of four little boys' jeans before I'd do the laundry and I'd find the most amazing things. Stones, nails, cool stones, screws, dead worms, old flowers, remains of crumbled cookies, crayons, pretty stones, pocket knives, 'pieces of money' (pennies, nickels etc.), sticks, pine needles, crumpled up pieces of paper, pine cones, stolen chocolate chips, white stones, pencils, erasers, candy wrappers, stones, string, scissors, stones streaked with minerals, rubber bands, etc.

And I thought it would be cool to label and date every single one of them for years and then, one day, put them out for display. That way, you could see what kinds of things little boys collect and how things they are interested in change as they grow older.

I did keep track for some time. But doing the task along with doing the laundry became endless and therefore was overwhelming. Besides which, it got to the point where I didn't have room to keep all the found treasures after a while.

Such is life, I guess.

13. Random Thought

Q : How do you make thirty eighty-year-old ladies all say the F word at once?
   A: Be the first one to yell, "BINGO!"

14. In Stitches

Years ago, I sliced my knee open lengthways with a can lid (long story). And because knees are meant to bend, there was NO WAY that my knee wasn't going to open up every time I moved it without stitches, so off to the ER I went. My son Hunter, fourteen at the time, came with me.

The next thing that happened was that the hospital made a grave mistake. They sat me in a newfangled wheelchair (the kind that goes every which way and can even turn corners when you're sitting still) *without any adult supervision.* I had a BALL as Hunter sat on a bench waiting patiently for his mother to sew her wild oats and settle down.

Before said wild oats were fully sown, a nurse came and found me and started asking me questions about my knee. Then she looked at Hunter (who looks A LOT like his daddy and almost nothing like me) and asked, "Is this your son?" to which I replied with a straight

24

face, "No, I've never seen him before! He was sitting here when I started playing in the wheelchair!"

I thought that the nurse was going to faint. She didn't know what to do with an unaccompanied minor when there was no adult around with whom she could think to put him. She stared at him, agog for a moment. Once she regained her faculties, she started questioning him about why he was there. Being my child, Hunter played along with it for as long as he could, until we both burst out laughing!

Pretty sure I've got a lifelong ban from that hospital.

15. Eme's Eggs

My lovely neighbors gave me a dozen eggs recently. On the carton, there was a note that read: "Eme's Egg Farm. Fresh eggs from free-range chickens (protected by Stewy and Biscuit, roosters-at-large)."

I am so charmed by this.

16. Forgive Thy Neighbor

I'm very sorry to report that my Jolly girl killed one of my wonderful next-door neighbor's chickens today.

Apparently, Stewy and Biscuit, roosters-at-large, did not count on Jolly when they were making their plans on how to best protect their girls.

Eme's mother told me this upsetting news, knowing it was important that I know, but nine-year-old Eme begged her mom not to tell me because even though she was upset, she said she "still loves Jolly..."

Recently I had a conversation with a teenager I know. She told me the story of her life, confiding in me some of her struggles as well as those of her family.

Among other things, as a young girl, she had to care for her younger siblings because her very young mother wasn't ready to be a parent. Then her father married a woman with children of her own, and he became so involved with them, he unwittingly neglected his own. She told me how she'd overcome some unimaginable heartaches, then added, "I will never hate my parents for what they did to me, I can't."

These two experiences came to me on the same day, and due to their juxtaposition, I found myself thinking about forgiveness and how it can be such a complicated business.

The nine-year-old, much as she grieved for her chicken, still saw the goodness in the dog that killed it and loved the dog in spite of her loss.

The seventeen-year-old I know who, after having an *extremely* difficult childhood, is still able to look at her very flawed parents and say, "I will never hate you for what you did to me."

It makes me wonder about the power and flexibility of forgiveness. And about our ability to forgive, if not forget. Why are some people able to forgive heinous crimes? Why are others not able to forgive minimal things? I don't have the answers to these and so many of life's other persistent questions, but I suspect that in the end, it all comes down to love.

For whatever the reason is, I am grateful that there are so many people in this world who can forgive generously. It makes the world a much better place to be!

17. Unexpected Aquifers

I magine my surprise when I discovered water reservoirs in my garden beds.

The indentations are relatively deep and slightly oval and hold a good amount of water. They look as though whatever made them could weigh as much as sixty-five pounds.

Why, that's almost as much as Jolly weighs, imagine that!

But no, no, no, no, nooo, she wouldn't go racing through her mother's garden faster than a greyhound chasing after a squirrel, tearing up some of her plants, and leaving footprint reservoirs. Nah, she would never do a thing like that.

18. The Fabric of Our Lives

T aking Jolly for a walk the other day, I looked out over the hillside and saw what appeared to be a huge patchwork quilt, sewn as if with bits and pieces of fabric in warm colors—brilliant red, glowing gold, bright orange, and shimmery pink—intertwined with varying shades of green. When putting them together, nature made an incredible whole.

Seeing this made me think of how so many interesting, yet mismatched fragments of experience are somehow stitched together to make the whole fascinating, rich, fabric of our lives.

19. Snagged

My mum was the absolute love of my dad's life, so her death practically destroyed him. He was grieving to the point where he couldn't bear the thoughts of collecting her ashes because that would have given her death a certain finality that he couldn't face.

Eventually, *six years* after her death, our upstairs neighbor and dearest family friend, Barbara, said, "Nancy, I think it is well past time to get those ashes, don't you?" So off we schlepped to the funeral parlor to "retrieve" my mother. I brought the ashes home, put them in a safe place, and said nothing to my father for fear of upsetting him.

A couple of years later, and unbeknown to me, Dad decided that he was finally ready to get Mom, only to discover that I'd already done so. Thereupon, he asked me for the ashes, at which point, I started to panic. Because if you know me at all, then you know that when I put things in a "safe place," it's a *very* safe place—as in never-to-be-seen-again safe.

And so, I searched. And searched. High and low.

I searched in my dad's apartment. I searched in Barbara's apartment. I searched in the storage bins in the basement. I even searched in my apartment (even though I *knew* she wasn't there).

All for naught.

Over the next few months, my dad asked me several times for the ashes, and I put him off, with "I'm so sorry, Daddy, I've just been really busy, but I *will* get them for you."

By this time, I was *really* in a panic because there was *no way* I could tell my father I'd lost my mother. What to do?

Well, living in Brooklyn at the time, I turned to the *only* solution I could think of and decided to have a BBQ on my fire escape using the hibachi grill and substitute *those* ashes for my mother's. *Great idea,* except, as it turns out, BBQ ashes *smell* like BBQ ashes until hell freezeth over.

So, I started adding baking soda to the BBQ ashes a little at a time to neutralize the smell. Turns out, it takes a *lot* of baking soda to neutralize that odor. Soon I found myself wondering if human ashes looked anything like what I had concocted, and I began praying Dad didn't *look* at them.

Then I bought an empty paint can (because ashes come in a container that looks like a plain paint can) and I put the open can full of BBQ ashes and baking soda on my fire escape to try to air them out more, and I prayed it wouldn't rain.

My next hurdle was the fact that (at the time anyway) you *had* to have a death certificate accompanying the can of ashes to bury them, and the funeral home had already procured one for us from the authorities. Once a death certificate is issued, that's it. You don't get another one. Except somehow, I did, although it was so long ago now that I don't remember *how* I did it, only *that* I did.

Eventually, armed with a plain paint can full of ashes and an accompanying legitimate death certificate, I presented my father with my "mother" and life was good. *Whew,* I thought, *crisis averted.*

Fast forward a year or so to when I got a phone call from my dad who said, "Nance, I've got a question for you. What exactly did you give me in that can? I just found your mother in the closet!"

Oops. Snagged!

20. Pigpen

Worse than this wicked heat is that it's super humid and the barometric pressure sky high!

So, there I was in my pumpkin garden, weeding and feeding the plants a combination of eggshells and coffee grounds that I'd been saving since November for plant food. The sweat was pouring off me, which meant the dirt, mulch, and eggshell mixture was stuck to me when a deer fly started a vicious attack. I tried swatting him away to no avail.

When I did finally get him, he'd landed in my hair, and I smacked him with hands that were caked with dirt, sweat, and old eggshell, adding fly guts to the mixture.

All I can say is *thank goodness* for running water.

Anyone who believes that man, bear, or big cats are the greatest predators on earth obviously have never encountered deer fly.

21. Stepping Back in Time

L ast night, we went to dinner at a local diner in our small town, and as we sat there, I could feel some of the day's stress start to ebb away. You see, stepping into this place was like stepping back to Mayberry at a simpler time. The decorations, wallpaper, carpet, lunch counter, even the tables, and chairs, spoke of bygone days. And the waitress wasn't some young hottie. Rather she was a warm, welcoming, attractive middle-aged woman, a little on the plump side, who called you honey and radiated a homey sense of Mom and love.

Adding to the feeling of stepping back was the kitchen staff's good-natured chatter about local folks, fishing, weather conditions, sugaring, and so on—all audible owing to the fact the kitchen wasn't locked away behind a swinging door; there was a large window where bountiful plates of well-cooked comfort food were being passed through to the waitresses.

To top it off, the radio was playing Kenny Rogers' "Ruby Don't Take Your Love to Town," The New Seekers' "I'd Like to Teach the World to Sing," and Linda Ronstadt's "Long Long Time," all hits of the late '60s and early '70s.

I wish that I'd had room for dessert, as the diner's offerings of things like Cherry Pie, Coconut Cream Pie, and Shoofly Pie sounded wonderful, like something Aunt Bea would make.

I don't go out to eat often, but I will most definitely go back there, especially when I'm feeling the need to step back in time!

22. Part of the Furniture

Years ago (I'm guessing fifteen), somebody gave us a big, overstuffed wingback chair. It's the kind of chair you can curl up in or sit cross-legged in comfortably if you're little like me. It was already third-hand when we got it, and the previous owner had dogs who'd claimed it. Consequently, when it got to us, it smelled like old, stinky dogs, and we instantly christened it the "dog chair."

The funny thing about the dog chair is that it is, well, "part of the furniture," if you know what I mean. But the fact is, being in its third family for at least fifteen years, a household with lots of boys, and coming to us from a household with several dogs, it's beyond ratty; it's downright falling apart. The arms have *long* since lost their fabric and quite a bit of their stuffing, and in places are down to the bones now.

So today, I got another, this time new, big, overstuffed chair. When asked where I was going to put it, I suggested, "Well, why don't we replace the dog chair with it?"

Holy smoke, you should have heard the ruckus! I was told in no uncertain terms, "The dog chair is *not* leaving! End of story."

Isn't it funny how ratty old things can claim such a large part of our hearts?!

.

23. In Her Dreams

It's funny to watch Jolly when she sleeps. So often you can tell she's dreaming of squirrels because her feet start going and she starts to whimper a little. It turns out she's a squirrel dog and day after day after day she looks out two of my windows where there is a large pine tree. Near the bottom of the tree, there are several broken-off branches where a pair of resident squirrels (we now have to abbreviate the spelling of that word to SQUs when we talk about them, or she knows what we're saying) sit comfortably and torment her.

And of course, the moment we let her out, she zooms around the house in hot pursuit of those SQUs who gleefully run up the tree.

I don't mean to sound unkind, especially since she's never actually caught a squirrel, but I think of how lucky she is to be dreaming of the thing she loves best to do, even if the only time she ever catches them is in her dreams.

24. Bilingual

I don't like to brag, but I am fairly fluent in "dog." I think I developed this skill because I had four babies, and of course, babies, like dogs, can't talk to tell you what they need or what is wrong, so you pretty much have to figure it out *why* they're crying *this* time.

I've found this same technique works well with dogs. For instance, when Jolly wants either food or water, she bangs her dish. That one's pretty easy. If she wants something else from me, she'll stick her nose under my arm. If she wants attention, she'll stay there. If she wants me to follow her, she'll nose me and then back away. Then it's up to me to figure out what she wants. Could be, she wants to go outside or to play, or one of her toys is stuck, and she can't get it out, or somebody's here, and she's excited, or she's hungry. (She doesn't always bang her bowl).

Then there is the scratching. When Jolly wants to be scratched, she leans against me, offering me different parts of her body: head, belly, midsection, and her butt.

Yup, Jolly, like so many critters do, loves to have her butt scratched.

Ah, the joys of motherhood.

25. Misinformation

There I was, picking cherry tomatoes and allowing my mind to wander, and of all the places it could have gone, I found myself thinking about how *Children suck the brain cells from your head.*

"And *why* were you thinking about that, of all things?" you are undoubtedly asking yourself.

The answer is simple. After being a parent for twenty-five years and raising four boys, my brain is now the size of a pea—or maybe (if I'm very lucky) as big as the small cherry tomatoes I was picking.

As further proof, I offer you this: You know that pop, pop, popping sound you hear as a pregnant woman walks by? Well, that's her brain cells leaping from her head. Because losing them, unquestionably, begins with conception!

And the loss of brain cells speeds up exponentially with each successive child you have.

Don't believe me? Ask *any* mother who has multiple children. I am *confident* she will *testify*!

And there you were, thinking it was only the aging process.

26. Music to Our Ears

I love goose song. I don't know why, but I do. Maybe it's the cadence or the often two notes sung. Maybe it's the sound of freedom or the heralding of the passing of time, signifying, "We're back!" in the spring or "Heading South, for now, see you next year" in the fall. Maybe it's because sometimes there is a solo and sometimes a chorus of voices.

Whatever the reason, I *love* goose song.

And when geese are flying overhead in a V formation, singing, if they are low enough, you can also hear the sounds of their wings, almost like a whisper coming from the heavens, which is also music to my ears and balm to my soul.

It occurred to me the other day that I'm not the only one in my family who loves goose song. Jolly does too! You might ask, rolling your eyes, "*How* on earth could you possibly know that?!?" Well, the answer is easy.

You see, North gave Jolly a stuffed goose that had a squeaky inside of its body. She loved it so much, she played and played and played with it until she destroyed it. But you should have seen her *delight* when she realized there was another squeaky in its head!

Squeak, squawk, squeak, squawk. Proof positive.

27. Bugged

Last night I went to a music jam and, as I was standing there, my right side kept tickling me as though a bug was crawling on me. I kept trying to find the bug and sweep it away, to no avail. *Argh!*

Then it hit me; it wasn't a bug at all. My friend Scott had just changed his guitar strings and hadn't clipped them. It was his strings that kept touching my side as he moved that tickled me!

LOVE getting the heebie-jeebies for no reason. Really.

28. Life Is Good

I've never grown corn before, so I had no idea how to tell if the corn was ready. Yes, I knew that corn silk turning brown was an indication, but now I know it's NOT the only one. Browning is only the first step. Next, the husks have to look a little papery.

But I've discovered that the most important indicator is the last one, which is when the cobs have pulled away from the stalks, sticking out like Alfalfa's ears on *The Little Rascals.*

For the last few days, I've been having a ball going out to the garden and inspecting my corn—both Indian and Pop. And every time I see a cob pulled away from the stalk, I joyfully run over and take it off.

The best part is sitting on my front porch pulling back the husks. It's akin to unwrapping a birthday present and seeing what's on the inside. Will I find rich mahogany cobs? Pretty speckled, multicolored kernels? Something mostly yellow, randomly dotted with various colors? Or perhaps the largely purple ones with creamy stripes? Happily, my popcorn is multicolored in so many different and interesting combinations.

And another really good thing: Readying time is as individual as the cobs themselves. So, this season of unwrapping the corn will continue for some time. YAY!

Life is good.

29. Fire the Housekeeper

Jolly is not what you'd call a good housekeeper. Honestly, she's more like a toddler. Meaning, while she's *very good* at taking her toys *out* of her toy basket, she's *lousy* at putting them back *in*. She *never* puts her toys away. Rather, she leaves them lay where she drops them, as I said, like a toddler.

With that in mind, I was in the kitchen in the wee hours yesterday morning, just turning on the light over my stove to start my tea water when I kicked one of the toys, which was laying against my stove on the floor. I sighed with resignation and said out loud, as I bent to retrieve it, "Jolly, WHY don't you ever clean up your toys?"

Only to find that her "toy" was a pair of one of my boys' skivvies.

I didn't ask. I don't think I want to know.

30. A Rustic Stool

In my kitchen, I have a small, dark brown, wooden stool. Although it is very well built, it is a very primitive stool that reminds me of something you might find in the middle ages—except for it having four legs, not three.

Silly as it may sound, I love that stool and use it all the time—partly because I am under-tall and need to stand on something to reach everything that is out of reach (which is most things in my life). And partly because it is the perfect height for me to sit on if I'm doing something like peeling and slicing apples or giving the dog some attention.

The stool lives in the corner where my sink and counter come together. Every time I sit there (which happens frequently), I feel like Cinderella—you know, "in my own little corner in my own little chair . . ." Thankfully, I can amuse myself.

Better yet, I am easily amused!

31. A Mother's Love

The other day, I had the pleasure of introducing my friends Annie and Audra to each other. As the three of us stood there chatting, I started laughing to myself because anybody who glanced at us, and was paying attention, would *immediately* know that we are mothers. All three of us were standing, gently swaying back and forth as if we were holding babies in our arms.

Thankfully, once a mother, always a mother.

32. Into the Wild

My grass out front is long. It started that way because we discovered loads of tiny little wild strawberries and I couldn't bear to mow them down, and so the grass got long, and I kind of like it that way.

The interesting thing is it doesn't look like a hayfield; rather, it looks like a meadow. The grass, though tall, is actually sparse and there are all kinds of pretty flowers in it: daisies, purple clover, Queen Anne's lace, and fox and cubs, for instance; and interesting weeds: St. John's wort, yarrow, wood sorrel, white clover, and curly dock, to name a few.

It's making my boys *nuts* not to mow it, but I *like* having a meadow.

33. Moonlight Musings

I was up at 2:43 am this morning because Jolly woke me, needing to go out. As I walked into the kitchen, I realized I didn't need to turn on a light because the moonlight was pouring through my windows so brightly that it lit my way with its silvery glow! As I stepped outside with the dog, I could smell the scent of night-time earth—did you know it has a different scent than daytime earth? —and the moon was so bright it threw everything in its path, including our outbuildings and vehicles, the trees on our property, and even distant mountains, into relief.

It is on quiet, bright nights like these that I think of all the people throughout history who, for one reason or another, traveled at night. Some perhaps were crossing deserts, *much* cooler at night, and would have been blessing the brightness of the moon for lighting their way. Others, such as slaves traveling the Underground Railroad, might have been cursing the moonlight; for even as it lit their way, it was so bright there also were few shadows to hide their movements.

Funny how simple things like moonlight can trigger an avalanche of thought.

34. Real-Life Rockwell

Driving along the other day, I passed a well-kept, white, wooden church by the side of the road with a maple tree in the front yard that was partly light green fading to gold, partly orange turning to crimson (how do they do that?), and partly already "bald."

Next to it sat a house with orange pumpkins, round, oblong, large, and small, on its descending front steps and the obligatory corn stalks on its uprights.

Just then, a pickup truck with a *towering* stack of hay drove past, and all I could think was, *I've just stepped into a Norman Rockwell painting!*

Life is good.

35. What's in a Name?

I have a pet peeve—well, lots of them, but this is the one on my mind at the moment.

I gave my four boys the strongest, male names I could think of: Forrest, Hunter, Wilder, and North. So, what's the peeve? I either know or know of girls with three of those names: Hunter, Wilder, and North. Really?

For the record, I am one who *genuinely appreciates* strong women, but I'm here to tell you, femininity doesn't have to be absent for a woman to be a strong woman!

I *also* appreciate strong, capable men and love genuine masculinity. I don't mean *machismo* here. Nor do I make the mistake of substituting *strong* for *disrespectful* or *controlling*.

Sadly, I think there are folks with an ax to grind; hence, they're giving their girls male names.

I say, allow your daughters to have beautiful, feminine names and teach them to be strong, capable young women so they can have the best of both worlds. And allow men the dignity of their masculinity!

36. From the Bottom of My Heart

There are few things we can do that are as gracious as sending a heartfelt thank you note. Nor are there many things we could do that would be more appreciated.

I've done all kinds of nice things for people, and I've been *lucky* if I have received a thank you note. And perhaps equally as bad are the ones that are so perfunctory. I'm not entirely sure why people bother to send them at all, things like preprinted notes that say, "Thank you for the gift." Really? Wow, that was heartfelt. Not.

Sadly, the art of a handwritten, lovely, heartfelt thank you note seems to have disappeared and I, for one, think it's time to bring it back! Think about it for a moment: If somebody gives you something or does something nice for you, they are in essence, taking time and money away from their own lives that they could use for the benefit of themselves or their families, and *that* is quite a gift.

Albeit kicking and screaming, my boys have been made to write thank-you notes all their lives, although thankfully, these days, they finally see the reason for doing so and will write them of their own accord, if not happily, at least knowing it is the right thing to do!

Next time somebody invites you to supper, remember that they've traded their time and labor for the money that purchased the food they've shared with you. Or if somebody thinks about you and spends precious time looking for, or making, a gift they believe you would enjoy—when they do, show them how grateful you are by writing a *heartfelt* thank you note.

Believe me. It will make a difference.

37. Time Management

As once again, Jolly woke me in the wee hours of the morning to let her out—and then took off—I am reminded of an old joke.

A time-management expert was driving past a farm where he saw a farmer with a pig in his arms, holding it up to a tree branch to eat individual apples it indicated it wanted by pointing with its snout. The pig would take a couple of bites then choose another apple, thereby repeating the process.

Crazed by the time waste of this act, the expert pulled over, ran up to the farmer, and said, "Look, I know it's none of my business, BUT the way you're feeding apples to that pig is an incredible waste of time! It would be soooo much faster if you shook a bunch of apples down from the tree and allowed the pig to walk around eating whichever apples it wants!"

The farmer looked at the time management expert, scratches his head, and says, "Well, I dunno. What's time to a pig?"

38. The Dance

Yesterday morning I walked into my bedroom to find a bright scarlet cardinal sitting on a lilac branch right outside my window. I looked at him and he at me, and then he started to sing. Since singing is what I do, I sang right back to him. He watched and listened as I sang. When I stopped, he flew away. But when I started to sing again, he came right back.

We danced this dance of music many times before I finally had to move on with my day, and it was most definitely gratifying to have a songbird enjoy my song!

39. Bird Brain

Hah! Remember when I told you about the bright scarlet cardinal with whom I shared various songs? It turns out he didn't give a hoot about my singing to him. Since then, he's come back almost every day to sit on the branches of the lilac, singing occasionally, but mostly attacking the window as if he's trying to get in.

I'm not sure if he's seeing his reflection and believes he's attacking a rival cardinal or if he thinks he sees bugs that look tasty. Or if it's a plain matter of him being a lunatic.

My money is on the latter possibility.

Ah well, once again my hopes and dreams are dashed! Which makes me wonder: Who's the real "birdbrain" here?

40. Roots and Wings

As a young child, starting around the age of three, it seemed that Fourth of July celebrations were just about the best thing about life. I can remember going to the local bandshell, where families, young and old, would congregate on the lawn, some sitting in the grass, others on blankets that moms brought. And there was a smattering of folding lawn chairs with brightly colored webbing that older folks sat on whose joints were a little too creaky for the lawn.

The concerts always started with "The Star-Spangled Banner" when all and sundry stood and sang, with their hands over their hearts, their voices swelling up to the heavens as a collected offer of allegiance, love, and pride.

And after the opening, while it was still light, children would run back and forth to the playground set in the sand between the concert lawn and the Great South Bay of Long Island, whose waves lapped soothingly against the shore. There would be swinging, riding "horses" atop super-thick, heavy-duty metal springs, or getting themselves dizzy on the merry-go-round, their laughter melding with the music, as if to say, this is an integral part of the music!

I remember snuggling with my parents as it got dark and feeling such a sense of love and belonging as I sang at the top of my little lungs along with the rest of those assembled to John Phillip Sousa's "Stars and Stripes Forever." This song always was perfectly timed to end just as the fireworks display began—a double treat to be sure, as the shimmering, sparkling, colorful lights reflected in the water to the oohs and ahhhs of the appreciative audience.

And when I couldn't possibly imagine anything better, we'd top off the evening with sparklers my daddy lit with his pipe lighter. My sister, brother, and I would wave around the almost-magical, shimmering, sparkling sticks in the dark. And then, heaven on earth, if we were very good, there might also be an ice cream treat from the Good Humor truck afterward.

The reality of life is that there is so much we *cannot* do for our children, especially once they are full-grown. But we sure can give them wonderful childhood memories to look back on.

Life is good.

41. Story of My Life

There I was last night, belting out "Angel from Montgomery" at one of my favorite places to play when some of the guys at the bar started cheering wildly! I. Was. THRILLED! I was *beyond* elated—until I realized they were watching Game Seven of the World Series!

Such is my life.

42. Moonshine Blues

Yesterday was a beautiful, almost summer's afternoon. The temperatures were in the low seventies, the sky was blue, there was a lovely breeze—not too light, not too strong—and I was on my way, singing in the car. I was pulled up to a T in the road and was turning onto the main road when, WHAMO, the cop that sits on the corner, flipped on his lights and nailed me.

He politely walked over to my window and said, "Well, ma'am, it sounds like your exhaust system is a little loud. As in, maybe it's not even attached?!" (Untrue. Well it *is* a little loud, but *not* like it's unattached!) I explained to him that my son's been driving the car, and I just took it out for the afternoon, so I really didn't know—and besides which "it is a silver car."

He looked at me in disbelief and said, "Pardon me?"

I replied with a smile, "It's a silver car." Then I pointed out the "black truck" and the "maroon SUV" that had just passed. He was looking at me like I had three eyes, so I explained, "I don't know *squat* about vehicles. All I can tell you is this is a silver car!"

Then he inquired, "Excuse me, ma'am, but have you been drinking?"

I told him that *no*, I didn't drink. Or smoke. Or drug. That I was, in fact, a weenie!

He said, "Where are you heading?"

I replied that I was off to sing (conveniently neglecting to tell him it was at a microbrewery) and pointed to my guitar.

He asked me for my license, "Just to see if there's anything on it." I gave it to him. As he walked away, *that's* when my eye fell on my mason jar full of water, and I started to laugh.

In no time, the policeman was back with my (clean) license. I held up the mason jar and asked, "Is *this* why you thought I'd been drinking?"

He said, "Well, I *did* notice the jug, and I wondered."

I laughed and told him it was water, then opened the lid and said, "Would you like to smell it or taste it?" He looked at me for a moment and replied, "Actually, ma'am, if you'd been drinking moonshine, I'd have been able to smell it from ten feet away! Sorry to bother you, have fun singing and have a good day!"

As he went, I called out, "Thank you for trying to keep folks safe and have a good day!"

Chalk another one up to the mason jar.

43. Civic Duty

I went to the local big-box store the other day, and as I was getting out of the car, I glanced over at the passenger seat where my gaze fell on my mason jar full of water. It occurred to me that I'd best hide it because if the local hillbillies saw it, they'd think they'd hit pay dirt, break into my car, and happily abscond with what they would assume to be a half-gallon of 'shine!

And I can only imagine that when they realized it was water and *not* 'shine it would tick them off that somebody had played a such a dirty trick on them, and they'd be likely to break the jar in frustration!

Whoever would have thunk that you'd have to hide a mason jar full of water to protect the good people of the town's tires?

44. Twenty-Four Hours of Blonde

The last twenty-four hours have, shall we say, been interesting. Starting with the 3:30 am vacuuming of my ear. There was a bug stuck in my ear canal for an hour and, after trying every other thing I could think of, I resorted to sucking the bug out using the vacuum hose.

Then I was outside in my garden and had been tying tomatoes up for an hour. I was on my second to the last stake and gingerly reaching for a wayward stem when, WHAMO, I hit myself in the eye with the stake. I was so intent on reaching that darned stem I didn't see the stake. Ahhh, try to see the Forrest through the trees.

Yep, another blonde moment. (If the village calls looking for the idiot, please tell them I'm on my way!)

Then Jolly found something horrifically stinky to roll in (what *is* it with dogs and stinky things anyway?), so of course, I had the dubious pleasure of bathing her.

And Jolly is not like so many of those doggies you see who *love* baths. Oh no. She—like my boys when they were little—*hates* baths. On top of that, she was *so* stinky that the peppermint soap I used did *nothing* to diminish the stink.

Ultimately, I resorted to using some of North's shampoo, which now has Jolly smelling like a French whore!

Oh yay.

45. So Blessed

I'd like to be able to say that I am always grateful for my many blessings, but that would be dishonest of me. The truth is, while I am *usually* grateful, there are times I take things for granted or wish things were different.

Examples of the kinds of things I'm talking about are: I live in a place that is warm and snug and keeps my family safe and sheltered, where I can have a big garden—and yet there are times I wish I lived in a different or "better" place. And at this point, I make my living in a kitchen and music is my hobby—but I'd give *a lot* to reverse that.

Late last night, I remembered I still had clothes hanging on the line. As I was outside in the warm summer's air, with fireflies twinkling all around me, I found myself thinking about the nature of gratitude and desire because I just got word that a schoolmate with whom I'd recently reconnected had died from cancer.

As I folded the blue jeans against my chest, I got a whiff of the clean fabric that had dried in the sunshine and summer breeze, and I knew I was one of the lucky ones. Tomorrow I would have another chance to smell the freshly laundered clothes right off the line, to watch the fireflies twinkle, to sing and cook, to sip another cup of hot tea sweetened with milk and honey as I was writing in the early morning, and to love my family and friends at least one more day.

I am so blessed.

46. Pie Crust Gadgets

I made a Strawberry Rhubarb pie the night before last. I was inspired to do it by the rhubarb growing in my yard. And while I had to purchase strawberries at the supermarket, I cut the rhubarb fresh right out of the patch beside my house and used it immediately.

As I reached into my utensil drawer for my lattice crimper, I got to laughing. You see, mine is not one of those lovely, fancy-schmancy lattice crimpers, the kind that "Every good cook *must* have" (said without moving your jaw); rather, mine is an old, plastic Play-Doh crimper toy. It's got a yellow shank and on one end a bright red wheel with square "teeth" and on the other a bright orange wheel with triangular "teeth" that leave jagged patterns. It seems like I've had it forever, but if memory serves, I bought it at a yard sale for a dime twenty years ago.

I did eventually buy a proper (and oh so fancy) lattice crust crimper, but truth be told, it doesn't work nearly as well as the old, go-to Play-Doh crimper so that one sits in my utensil drawer.

Funny the kinds of things that come into our lives that we become attached to, isn't it?

47. Oil Cans

I *love* old oil cans. And yes, I mean the kind the Dorothy used on the Tin Man in *Wizard of Oz*. I know it sounds crazy, but the fact is they are cool and beautiful, come in all sorts of shapes and sizes depending on their intended purpose, and they are dead useful!

I can picture an old farmer in a ball cap needing a big can with a very long nozzle to get to some part in the bowels of a piece of farm equipment, or an old-time clock maker needing a teeny, tiny one with a very delicate spout.

Some are tin, others copper or brass. Some are painted red or green. Then there are those with handles sprouting off their sides big enough for a large hand to grasp firmly, or delicate enough that you'd think you were drinking tea with the Queen, using tiny, fragile teacups—pinky up, of course. Some have a flexible bottom that you press, and it releases the oil.

And their spouts—big, fat, tiny, petite, loooonnnng, short, bent, jointed, straight—I can't seem to help myself, every time I see one, I'd like to take it home, start a collection and display it on a shelf.

Once a tomboy, always a tomboy, I guess.

Sheesh.

48. It's All Greek to Me

Last night, I realized that a guitar player (yours truly) trying to jam with a bunch of mandolin players when she doesn't know the song so that she's watching their hands, is like a person trying to read lips that are speaking a foreign language!

Yeah, what you said . . .

49. Wildflower Bouquets

When my boys were little, they would delight in finding some wildflowers, pick them, and come to me with their hands behind their backs to hide their gift until they could properly present them to me. And I don't know who got more pleasure out of that—them for picking something so pretty for their mommy or me for having such a pretty, thoughtful gift given to me with such love.

Sadly, those days are pretty much gone, especially now they're grown with their own "girls" to give flowers. Thankfully, there is an occasional exception.

While it doesn't often happen, every once in a while, one of my boys still thinks to pick me wildflowers and present them to me.

Which means that right now, sitting on my kitchen sink windowsill, there is a little glass extract bottle holding a small bouquet of delicate purple and white violets. And I can't tell you how much pleasure I get, on so many levels, from looking at those beautiful little flowers!

50. Penny for Your Thoughts

Sad to say a penny isn't worth a red cent anymore. Some of it is that it costs more to produce them than they are worth—literally. Some of it too is that folks seem to find coins quite a bother, to the point where I've seen people take the change from their pockets and fling it across a parking lot.

And I can't tell you how many times I've seen people step over coins like quarters, nickels, and dimes, forget pennies because apparently, it's too much of a bother to pick them up.

Not me. There's something about finding a coin on the ground that gives me such joy that I *always* bend over and pick it up! I think that's because, for me, the value of a penny isn't the monetary value, but rather the joy it brings in finding one!

Once upon a time, a penny was worth something, and you could purchase all kinds of things with just one! And what you could get with a few of them—a bunch of other stuff. *Hoowee,* no wonder folks bent over and picked it up whenever they saw one!

Then too, there is the "good luck" aspect to it. As a kid, I was taught: "Find a penny heads up, pick it up for good luck!" Only for me, they're *all* good luck—no matter if they're heads up or tails up, ergo I *always* pick them up.

And if I'm with somebody when I find one? I *always* give the penny to them—that way I can share my good luck!

51. Voices Raised in Praise

Early this morning, I was up making a hot cup of tea when I heard coyotes singing. There were only two of them. One was yipping a steady rhythm, and the other would periodically chime in and howl. Yip, yip, yip, yip, yipyipyip, yip, then a howl, a moment's pause, and then yip, yip, yip, yip, yipyipyip, yip, and then another howl. They sounded quite joyful as they sang their duet over and over at the top of their lungs as though giving thanks to the Creator for the day.

Or perhaps they were summoning others because after a few minutes of hearing their song they were joined by at least two more. You could tell there were more because the voices were different and now two at a time were yipping while the other two were howling. They were singing four-part harmony.

I love to hear the voices of the critters. It both soothes and thrills me.

Life is good.

52. The Sink

Yesterday morning, before I left the house for the day, I made sure every single dish in the house was clean, the table and counters cleared off, and the sink empty.

When I came home, the sink was full, and there were dishes all over the counter.

Gosh, I *love* when that happens—almost as much as I love stubbing my pinky toe really, really hard.

53. For Love and Art

Random thought. The dichotomy of being a guitar player and the chief cook and bottle-washer is a dilemma. I need very short fingernails to play guitar, but that sure makes it hard to do things like grab an onion and hold it with your fingernails as you're trying to chop it quickly.

Sheesh, the things we do for love and art!

54. Lost in Translation

Does anybody speak "mouse"? Because we've tried *everything* (well, except poison) to get rid of the little buggers and they keep coming back. And to be frank, I don't have unlimited time to clean up after them, although why they should be any different than my boys, I don't know.

Anyway, If you *do* speak mouse, could you please tell me how to say, "So nice you enjoy my home and find it comfy and cozy, but I wish you'd stay your *dumb ass* the #%$!^#@ out of my house!!!"

Thanks, I would appreciate it.

55. Outdoorsmen

My boys are outdoorsmen through and through. That's how we raised them. Because of this, I have no issue with them keeping a worm container in my fridge.

I do, however, think that *seven* worm containers are a bit much—after all, the fridge is a relatively small box that is meant to keep food cold (not maintain the freshness of worms), which matters a good deal, especially since my boys like to eat—and I don't mean worms!

No doubt, I can live with seven worm containers in my fridge. It's the *empty* worm containers I can't live with!

Sheesh, what's next? Snakes? Bats?

56. Living Wrong

I *love* stone walls. Thankfully they are ubiquitous in the Northeast. There must be hundreds of thousands, maybe millions of miles of them, crisscrossing the countryside, built by hand and back, stones dug from fields and creeks, placed one by painstaking one, fitting them together as best they could. They are works of art in so many ways, and yet they had real purpose those walls. They kept livestock in and were a visual boundary to people.

Can you imagine these days slowing down enough to build all those walls by hand as our forefathers did? Me either.

I think we're living wrong.

57. Sunday Morning Pancakes

As a general rule, for the past twenty-plus years, Sunday morning has been Pancake Morning in our household. My boys *loved* pancakes. Plain, banana, wild blueberry (made from berries that we picked ourselves), and even occasionally, chocolate chip pancakes, which were smothered in butter and drenched with maple, sour cherry, blueberry, or elderberry syrup. They were such a treat that my little boys always looked forward to Sunday mornings.

Now that everybody's older, running in different directions, and not necessarily wanting breakfast, not to mention this heat and humidity we've had this spring (argh), we haven't had many Pancake Mornings lately. So, it was a great pleasure when North (my youngest son) asked me the other day if I would please make pancakes on Sunday morning. I did so joyfully, as I love my boys, and it took me right back to the best days of my life!

58. Floppy Dog Ears

There is something both appealing and irresistible about floppy ears on a dog! I find myself so drawn to them and can't seem to help myself as I scratch, rub, and flop their ears around.

Luckily dogs like it a lot when people do that.

I guess the Creator knew what he was doing when he gave dogs floppy ears.

59. Granny Knots

There is something about granny knots that I love. Somehow, I can envision a little old lady in an old house wearing an apron needing something to stay put and tying a granny knot to keep it in place, with the silent chant of "Good enough is good enough" and having a sense of satisfaction about the work she'd done.

I'm an old sailor from way back (and yes, I *can* cuss up such a storm, it would make an old salt blush). That still I am a sailor was brought home to me when I was tying up tomato plants using the Braille system (where you don't look). At first, I assumed I was tying them up using granny knots until I realized with a jolt that my hands were automatically making square knots.

If you're unfamiliar with tying square knots, the mantra is "Right over left, left over right." Probably the reason I hadn't realized I was making square knots by rote was that I was doing them backward—in other words, left over right, right over left.

I felt a certain sense of satisfaction when I realized what I was unconsciously doing, especially since square knots are far less likely to slip. Even so, the truth is, granny knots will always and forever hold a special place in my heart.

60. The Mothering Instinct

One of my boys works with a very handsome twenty-three-year-old young man. He's also very hardworking, polite, and what I would consider a "nice kid."

At some point, I started hearing stories about how this good-looking young man forgot to make lunch, and he'd be *starving* as the day progressed. I had occasion to talk to him at one point, and I said, "You know you really bring out the ... mothering instinct in me. You need to eat!"

You should have seen the look of horror on his face before the words *mothering instinct in me* registered.

I don't mean to be evil, but I can only imagine what he was thinking I was going to say and I'm *still* chuckling at the look of horror on his face.

61. Night-Blooming Nicotiana

For years I wanted to plant Night Blooming Nicotiana (Tobacco). I'd read about it, and it sounded so cool and wonderful, yet I never did. Finally, this year, when I placed my seed order, I treated myself and ordered a packet of Nicotiana seeds, though I had no idea what to expect.

Turns out, they grow long and leggy tiny little purple flowers that, come evening, give off the most amazing, heavenly scent!

I would highly recommend you plant them, even if it's in a flowerpot on your windowsill. Oh my gosh, you won't be disappointed!

62. Instant Karma

A friend and fellow gardener owns a store, which I was in last week when I ran into him. He was collecting some items that he needed for a project, and when his hands were full, he put them on a counter and walked away to fetch something else.

Well, the devil was in me (no surprises there), so, as he walked away, I quickly grabbed a couple of those items and brought them up front, to the register, thus hiding them in plain sight. While I was there, I noticed a basket of beautiful mini peppers he'd brought in that had a "FREE" sign on them, and I promptly scooped out two and took a bite out of one of them.

Oops! Turns out they were HOT ghost peppers.

Pretty sure that falls into the category of instant karma.

63. Jolly Girl

Jolly and I were out in the garden, checking on the corn. I was in and amongst the rows and Jolly was off somewhere out of sight, playing with a stick, when I started whispering, "Jolly. Jollllllly. Jolly girl, where is Mommy?" to get her going.

I didn't see her anywhere, so I repeated myself.

And when I *still* didn't see her, I figured I'd better go and find her to make sure she hadn't taken off. I turned around in the row to go out the way I came, and *that's* when I screamed a startled scream because, there she was, *right* behind me looking at me expectantly.

Yup, pretty sure *that* one also goes under the category of instant karma.

64. A Discerning Eye

Jolly is thrilled. Wilder has so kindly given her a "private stash" of sticks for her very own. He's been collecting them for some time now and has them neatly stacked next to the barn just for her. Large and small, fat and thin, she joyfully pulls one out whenever she wants to play stick, which is just about all the time!

A less discerning eye would almost think it looks like kindling and firewood stacked next to the barn and close to the fire ring. But not Jolly.

Jolly knows better.

Jolly has faith.

65. Mouths of Babes

When my boys were little, we tried to watch our language. Although the fact is, there were times, in sheer frustration, when we'd let a few cuss words fly. Of course, those *would* be the words that children seem to grasp, as they are flying out of our mouths, taking some of our frustration with them. Worse yet, my kids held on to these words for dear life as if they were precious gifts to be brought out and shown *only* when there was "special company," like grandparents visiting.

I don't remember the exact details, but at some point, Forrest (six at the time) decided that he had to protect his little brothers when he was talking about *those* words and, mimicking the adults around him, he would "spell them" by using all sorts of random letters.

There were lots of little spellings, but THE BIG ONE, the one he knew was REALLY BAD that meant *serious business,* he spelled E.O.P.O.S.O. Whew, that was rough.

66. Improvisation

I have a tip for you. Last week, I started to make Shortbread; only I got distracted and burned the butter. However, knowing of "Burnt Butter" recipes that are wonderful, I went ahead and put the dough together, and it was alright. It wasn't horrible, but nor was it wonderful.

Unsure what to do with it, I put the dough aside and let the decision of "what to do with it" percolate. Then, yesterday, I elected to make some additions (vanilla and almond extract along with some coconut and mini chocolate chips) and bake them.

It turns out, with all these additions, those cookies were still just "alright." They weren't terrible, nor were they stellar.

So, my tip? If you have cookies that are nothing more than "alright," leave them out on a plate where teenaged boys can see them, and they'll disappear like magic!

67. Biscuits and Baskets

I made Cowboy Breakfast this morning (specifically the same biscuits with sausage gravy that I used to make as a treat for my "cowboys" when they were little), and as I reached for the basket that holds the biscuits, a flood of memories came washing over me.

The basket, which is about fifteen years old and made of dark brown grapevine, is vaguely heart-shaped and hangs on my wall where I can have easy access to it. I *love* that basket, and I reach for it whenever I make biscuits, rolls, or scones.

But the thing that I love *most* about that basket is how I acquired it. You see, all those years ago, when my son Hunter was very little (he's now almost twenty-four and stands six-foot-six), we wove it together. It was a project he and I made together at a 4-H meeting. Only once he brought it home, he didn't know what to do with it. But I did.

For me, not only is this basket beautiful, but it's also a useful tool of life. And no matter what gets put in it, it will always hold a piece of my heart!

68. Patience

I was so excited. Not only did I inherit an asparagus bed—I got two of them! And we were told that there would be enough asparagus for several meals.

I couldn't wait until spring. And then, in no time, asparagus season started, and I did indeed get asparagus. One. Stalk. At. A. Time.

Over several weeks I might add.

Sigh.

69. Shine a Light

Jolly got me up at 3:30 this morning and I couldn't go back to sleep, so I made myself a cup of tea and sat down at the computer. At one point, I looked up and saw "the light" I instantly felt a sense of all being right with the world.

I'm usually up before the sun (even during the summer), and when I walk into the kitchen in complete darkness, I head for the stove and turn on the light that's just above it.

There's something about that light I adore. It's the only one I turn on when I'm up early, heating water to make my morning cup of tea. It's not a bright light— not by any stretch of the imagination—, rather it casts a warm, soft glow that is both comforting and beckoning.

I've frequently wondered if this is how the cavemen felt about fire: that a soft, warm glow, which not only enabled them to see but gave them heat as well, was the source of life for them during long dark winters.

Or perhaps an early settler, who'd put a candle in a window to welcome a weary family member home who was out late, or who was carrying the candle to check on the well-being of their children while they slept.

Fact is, I'll never know how the cavemen or early settlers felt, but somehow, I believe there is a thread of connection passed down from generation to generation and going way back to our caveman ancestors. And for some reason, I got caught in that thread.

70. Simple Pleasures

Few are the simple pleasures that equal picking sun-ripened cherry tomatoes right off the vine and popping them in your mouth. They're like tiny little jewels, bursting with a sweet/tart flavor.

The pleasure is compounded because they're warmed by the sun.

Life is good.

71. Country Living at Its Finest

One of the great pleasures of childhood in the country is walking barefoot in the grass. If you're very lucky, a flower will get caught between your toes as you walk along! But you haven't truly lived until you step in a fresh pile of dog poop barefoot.

Now, if you've never done so, you are likely saying, "Ewwwww, GROSS! THAT'S DISGUSTING!!!"

And if you *have,* right now you are LAUGHING AND NODDING YOUR HEAD, all the while saying, "Yup, it *is* disgusting!!!"

Ah, country living at its finest.

72. Singing to My Children

I *always* sang to my children. I couldn't help it if I wanted to, the music *always* just *poured* out of me, so I sang to them.

One of their favorites was "I Had a Rooster." Wilder particularly loved that song, and one day, when he was about two, he said to me, "Mommy, sing 'Woosta.'"

Wise guy that I am, I obliged him and sang, "I had a woosta, the woosta pleased me."

Wilder looked at me confusedly for a moment, then he stopped me and, in all seriousness, said, "Mommy, it's a woosta, *not* a woosta!"

Twenty years later, I *still* chuckle about that.

73. When Mom's Away

When I went to work earlier, I put some music on for Jolly to listen to (don't judge), and some really good stuff at that—folk-rock, roots, alternative country, and so forth.

When I got home, I realized that there wasn't any music playing, so I went to look and there, right in front of me on the console, was the headline: "Top Ten Songs to Strip To."

OMGOSH, I hope she's not scarred for life!

Guess it's time to reassess my playlists.

74. A Good Attitude

Sometimes when I get down, I find myself pondering life and how hard it can be. And I wonder, how much of having a good life is really about having a good attitude?

As an example, you can't help but know people, or at least know *of* people, who are doing all kind of fabulous things—people who travel to beautiful, exotic places; people who go to concerts and openings and wonderful, trendy restaurants; and people who are blessed enough to be living their dreams.

There also are those who own all sorts of stunning things, such as fancy cars, boats, apparel, jewelry, pieces of equipment, and beautiful homes—you can fill in the blanks for yourself—, but the point is, things *most* of the population only dream about owning.

And yet, often, even people blessed with such abundance are often unhappy.

I know a man who spent the majority of his life outdoors, going places and doing things, who is now a resident in a nursing home. When I asked after him, I was told that he's "really ornery." *No doubt* the man is feeling deprived of the things that used to bring him great joy. And make no mistake about it, the things that brought him joy were very, very simple pleasures.

But I wonder if he could find joy in other things now, like talking to new people, hearing their stories, teaching them all kinds of cool and interesting stuff?!?

My top three questions related to this issue are:

1. How much of having a good life is really about having a good attitude?

2. Is it attitude and *not* doing all kinds of fun things (or having all kinds of fancy stuff) that makes the difference with happiness? And,

3. *How* do you change your perspective from one of envy to one of gratitude, especially when you see all kinds of other people around you doing (and having) all sorts of things that you'd like to do (and have) but can't?

I guess maybe sometimes you've got to count your blessings and call it a day.

Life is good.

Acknowledgments

I want to thank all the people who for years, encouraged me to, "Write a book." If it weren't for you, I wouldn't have undertaken the task.

Cindy Snow-Pitts, Deborah W. Clark, John Brett, Jenna Lynn Gerrish, Wayne Levandoski, Merilyn Carey Donaldson, Tim Martin, Ralph Huntington, Laurie Cutler Kalanges, Renee Burke, Sharmon Gereg Dyer McKee, Marcia Sweeney-Young, Deborah Storrs, Sigurbjorn Marinosson (Sig Mar).

Thanks to Leslie Jackson who is the reason I started writing after she implored her friends, "Tell me about your day . . ." and so I did.

Thank you to my dear friend Jolene Pirrone, website designer extraordinaire, who has always stepped up to the plate to help me out and for knowing what needs to be done when I don't have the foggiest!

Thank you, Matthew Pirrone, for snapping the only good photo taken of me in twenty years!

Thanks to Gus Yoo for the beautiful cover design.

Thanks to John Ordover for suggesting I contact Stephanie Gunning.

And lastly though *far* from least, thanks to Stephanie Gunning, editor extraordinaire. Because without her wisdom and guidance, this book would NEVER have come to fruition!

TRULY I am blessed.

ABOUT THE AUTHOR

Nancy Carey Johnson is a singer/songwriter and hemp farmer living in Poultney, Vermont. She lives with her husband, four sons, and her dog, Jolly. In her spare time, she gardens and bakes.